pain
killer

poems written
2000-2006

Patricia Spears Jones

TIA CHUCHA PRESS
LOS ANGELES

ACKNOWLEDGMENTS

Grateful acknowledgment to the editors of the following journals and websites where these poems first appeared: 88: A Journal of Contemporary American Poetry, African Voices, Barrow Street, Black Renaissance Noire, Bomb, Crazy Horse, downtown Brooklyn: a journal of writing, No. 18. Hanging Loose 9, Heliotrope, Mosaics #18, nocturnes 3: (re) view of the literary arts, Ploughshares, Rattapallax 12, TriQuarterly, The Oxford American, The Poetry Project Newsletter, The Same, www.poetz.com and www.sandrapayne.com. And these anthologies: Bowery Women: Poems (YBK Publishers) and Poetry After 911: An Anthology of New York City Poets, (Melville House).

Trabajan la sal y el azucar/Construyendo una torre blanca?" and "Era verdad aquel aroma/de la doncella sorprendida" from the chapbook repuestas! (Belladonna Books).

I thank the New York Foundation for the Arts for grant support and the Virginia Center for the Creative Arts for a residency, where many of these poems were started. I am grateful for the generosity and hospitality of Linda Speer and Marcus Luck in upstate New York and Deborah Wood Holton in Chicago whose homes made great writing residences.

Every poetry collection has its angels and this one includes Mary Baine Campbell, Cyrus Cassells, Peter Covino, Thomas Sayers Ellis, Veronica Golos, Kimiko Hahn, Angela Jackson and Maureen Owen and Sandra Payne. Special thanks to Peter Covino, Fanny Howe and Nina Zivancevic for their poems which provide the conversational frame for this collection. And thanks to Carl Hazelwood for his beautiful art work.

And finally, thanks to the editorial and design crew at Tía Chucha Press: Luis Rodriguez continues to bring forth great collections by poets of color and Jane Brunette is a designer extraordinaire. I am glad to be among the chosen.

Printed in the United States of America

ISBN 978-1-882688-40-1

Book Design: Jane Brunette
Cover painting: "Black & White Angel" by Carl E. Hazelwood.
Cover background art and part open art: "Black Elegance" by Stephanie Junod.
Back cover photo: Thomas Sayers Ellis

PUBLISHED BY:

Tía Chucha Press
A Project of Tía Chucha's Centro Cultural, Inc.
PO Box 328
San Fernando, CA 91341
www.tiachucha.com

DISTRIBUTED BY:

Northwestern University Press
Chicago Distribution Center
11030 South Langley Avenue
Chicago, IL 60628

Tía Chucha Press is the publishing wing of Tía Chucha's Centro Cultural, Inc., a 501 (c) 3 nonprofit corporation. Tía Chucha's Centro Cultural has received funding from the National Endowment for the Arts, the California Arts Council, Los Angeles County Arts Commission, Los Angeles Department of Cultural Affairs, The California Community Foundation, the Annenberg Foundation, Thrill Hill Foundation, the Middleton Foundation, Not Just Us Foundation, the Weinberg Foundation, among others, as well as donations from Bruce Springsteen, John Densmore, Lou Adler, Richard Foos, Adrienne Rich, Tom Hayden, Dave Marsh, Mel Gilman, Jack Kornfield, Jesus Trevino, David Sandoval, Denise Chávez and John Randall of the Border Book Festival, Luis & Trini Rodríguez, and more.

To the memory of Peter Dee, David Earl Jackson, Jr. and Lorenzo Thomas whose writing, talk, loyalty, joy and decency continue to lift me up.

"One Love"

TABLE OF CONTENTS

three

four

CODA

This business of being human

should not be such a lonely proposition.

—LYNDA HULL, STAR LEDGER

PAINKILLER

I can taste the metal
lose my desire for red meat

relax, every muscle
relax
emotion
relax
the time of day
I can give you
the time of day
What I talk about is how
love eludes me
No what I talk about is
what's wrong with me

No what I talk about is
what will happen to me

Fear
is the secret.
Always fear.

What you get from me is
the edge of a trace of shadows
and that's all you'll get
I can't give anymore
I don't want to
Everything hurts

This hurtle into living space
and that swift slide out of it.

You want secrets
I say every reckless act
results from a moment of fear.
While compassion is the simple recognition

That what is done cannot be undone,
may not be forgiven.

And a recognition that the murderer and the martyr
the adulterer and the healer can at any moment
change positions, become the other.

It simply depends on how much pain
You need to kill.

ONE

And yet! There is so much room
for every single occurrence of idiocy
in one's own lifetime–providing you have
a life in your prime . . .

—NINA ZIVANCEVIC
DEATH OF NEW YORK CITY

What the First Cities were All About

Cylinder seal/lapis lazuli
Yes, all blue, all the time
beer drinking Mesopotamians
dancing to the music made on the bull-headed lyre

The best in time best in show
best to know that partying is ancient,
inexorable and A LOT OF FUN

But where is that bull-head liar?
With whom is he flirting?
And what is she wearing, breasts perfumed
gleaming curls, black eyes encircled by *kohl*?

And how did the pig become THE NEW BULL?
Or is he THE NEW DOG, canine, Roman,
that other world, not as old, but just as festive—
togas, pendants, wine and moon madness.

Where is Catullus' napkin?
Was it blue?

SPRING SNOW

Unlike the young lover in Mishima's *Spring Snow*,
I cannot trust your mouth's promised sweetness.
First love was long ago

On Brooklyn streets,
Cherry, apple and pear blossoms
Quiver in harsh wind

Darkness comes quickly as do snow unexpected
Heart's anger glistens, all roads are hazardous,
but take them, we must

THAT PAINTING AT THE MET

She looks like Carol DeForest, but according to signage
She's Mrs. Isaac Newton Phelps Stoke
dressed for motion—a boating party?

Her mate- Mr. Stoke, Mr. Phelps Stoke?- at her side,
bowler hat in hand
his stern posture on the verge of a slouch perhaps?

They are wealthy and perfectly turned out
for the ghostly geometry of Sargent's lucrative formula.

A century later Carol shares the bride's charisma
and her dark, generous eyes and healthy skin

Carol is happy to be moving in light, air, dust, mortal
but once was Mrs. Isaac Newton Phelps Stoke
alive in this double portrait, circa 1897, fearless,
comfortable, ready to watch

another sunset with her handsome husband
as America vaunts its first prerogative.

AUTUMN, NEW YORK, 1999

And I am full of worry I wrote to a friend
Worry, she replied about what— love, money, health?

All of them, I wrote back. It's autumn, the air is clear
and you hear death music—the rattle of leaves swirling

the midnight cat howling, a newborn baby's 3 am
call for food or help or heart's love

At the market, the green, red and yellow apples are piled high,
sweet perfume—once, I went apple picking in Massachusetts

a day of thralling beauty, my companions and I
had no desire to leave the valley—the plump trees,

the fierce pride of small town New England where a gift shop
exploded gingham, calico, silly stuffed toys

we stood within this shrine to cloying femininity of entwined hearts
and ribbons and bows like invading aliens, fascinated and appalled

and here too, people throng around the dahlias—
the last of the bright fat flowers. Open. Scentless.

It is going to be a very hard winter and we all know it in our bones
an almost atavistic memory with instruction—wear heavy clothes
horde food, drink water, stand against the wind

listen.

NEW YORK ACCENT

It's amazing how people can say all right
with no *els* in sight or sound

the *els* expelled from mouths large and small
old and young. *Aw ite*

The *els* have taken leave of New York
and moved to Birmingham
or Budapest or Ceylon
(is there a Ceylon?)

I miss the *els*
those two consonants lull around a speaker's mouth
soft and promising–all

right. But these displaced *els*
shun belief

that, indeed, yes, all right
is all and right. Word is knifesharp
irony conquers consonants

and I worry for the vowels like the *as*
in Manhattan. Heard them lately?

YOUNG GIRL, BIG CITY

Looking for the back story, nostalgia for that grim generosity
of New York mid seventies. Subway dirty. Chinatown cheap.
The impossible heels of Puerto Rican girls tottering.
Strung out drag queens dazzle on Halloween, shining like the stars
they knew they were.

You could breach a lifetime of disenchantment
just walking across 12th street, river to river.
How your jeans shuffled was up to you.
As was how you danced

in downtown lofts with well-made paintings by really good looking guys,
all of whom studied at Yale or Columbia or had been in the Peace Corps.
Did something. Adventurous.
Just, not the war.

Late 1999, a tall, fat Black woman wearing a canary yellow leather jacket
marches down Washington her Donna Karan sneakers glinting.
Local boys stand hooded, hawkish checking her,
then me, whomever walks alone.
Prey. Possibility.

Later you can hear the short fat sounds that real guns make.
Then the cops may drop down behind your building chasing the man
    bleeding.
He goes over the neighbor's fence, voiding blood and dope along the way.

How random shots connect—gang bangers outside night club
waiting for the young Black man of so many possibilities
cops subduing the bearded half-dressed schizophrenic in Boro Park
an elderly woman surprised by the junkie who borrowed a dollar
is an odd geometry, felt, not traced, like the pattern of stars seen by a myopic

Where the pretty young woman was murdered, there is fresh paint and
   ordinary sidewalk.
The candles and flowers gone.
Only in our minds now the "Memorial" for young girl life lost.

Her mortal wounds remind us, goodness is not a shield.
Regret honors not her full life stopped by a useless man
who walks around here feeling not one thing.
His life as fruitless as the cash he took, that lasts as long as he looks
across a diner's grimy table.

.

All Saints Day, 2001

The floating lights of the emergency vehicles circle wind.
We walk immune to Sirens shrieking.
What if the circling lights were pink or yellow, not blue and white?
Who is the Saint of fog?

                          Who is the Saint of
our city decelerated in thick humidity, intemperate heat?

                          Who is the Saint of
smiling eyed pretty girls wearing tiny heeled shoes and short skirts
prowling loud pubs on 2nd avenue or the gray hooded Black guys
smoking weed, talking trash in the shadows of Grand Central?

                          Who is the Saint of
the Black woman in the pizza parlor who, after too many noise complaints
unheeded, declares I own a 9 millimeter, legal,
if I shoot your dog what are you going to do about it?

                          Who is the Saint of
the boys in my "hood"
who call each other "son"
peer to peer father to father.

Where's daddy
Where's mama
Where's the good old days?

                                        Is this the new catechism
and where is the handsome priest to answer?
By rote: do we sing a possible peace?

Shall we venture into this destroyed world thinking
charm, glee, proverbial opportunity

Shall we gather the names of the lost
then watch them float like feathers on the dirty wind

Shall we gather at the altars of old gods
and whine about our lives

                                        Shall we watch the shadows watch us back

Now that clocks pulse instead of tick
are the streets safer for the wretched, the damned?

In what cinema are the dreams of mass destruction
so dear as ours?

TWO

"What did you say to him?"

—Nothing. I loved him.

—FANNY HOWE, GONE

SHIMMER

how fire begins is easily explained
that's why people hate science

who wants to know
the precise chemical composition of depression?
Can't there be mysterious forces
and the loss of shimmer?

when stars explode on summer evenings
must we match their bright fury
with the precise velocity of light?

Radio waves are a wonder to behold—
speech pulsing like sex with a new lover
and can't that be enough?

What I will miss is kissing in cabs

Even in my randy youth, I never so much as *made out* in public

But, you love kissing in cabs. You love moving bodies around in moving vehicles.

You have perfected the arc of command, solicitous, somewhat grand

in *the masculine manner.*

Working your hands down blouses, lifting skirts

Oh, it's your arms around my waist, your hand on the cool of my chest

your fingers squeezing my left nipple, your tongue down my throat,

that makes me worry about the psyche of taxi drivers.

Will the Russian get a hard-on, will the Haitian throw us out?

Will we make it across the Hudson, to home?

And who will pay dearly for this bad behavior

My Movie: A Suite

(in translation)

boca

baci

roses

you

much too late

why the midnight baritone on the telephone

when you must leave hours before dawn?

Tryst

on the IRT platform at Canal & Lafayette

my arms around your neck, I want your mouth

Your eyes laugh me in

Your hands ramble through my hair

Two girls behind us giggle their own important news

My *movie*

Waiting for me at the Grand Central Information kiosk

This is my movie, my instruction. He

slouches like Belmondo in *Breathless*

feline smooth, bear like growling

he has his woman in sight

what else does he need to do?

We ride up the escalator to what used to be

the Pam Am building, he feels me up.

One of us is blushing

Garlic, ginger, cilantro, salt

During lunch, he says

"I love lookin at you"

I drop my fork

Food sits in heaps.

Why silence is like a volcano

Four days,

     no word

     Fire from the mountain

        Lava makes new rivers

Hawaii is so near.

Tributary

between nipple and the cock's split tip,

melanin fleshes a deeper, darker brown

pleasure and genesis at play

nappy hairs circle and re-circle

your skin's sweat to taste my mouth

seeks all your earth bound beauty

torso and groin   Oh tributary

splash

Waiting for the year of the horse

a full moon or the shape of its coming

day after my birthday, horse gallops in

the lunar year—no more dragons, are we happy

will there be fire crackers, shouts in the streets, curses

Oh demons be gone!

are you the rider I expected or a messenger with bad news

am I your sanctuary or a difficult harbor to navigate

your hands are large enough to hold many things

and to let them loose

one by one

rose petals

coins

my name in metal

explode

Son Cubano

We are at the genesis of a *bolero*
eyes, lips, thick, kinky dreads
beds, cars, stars

a singer's words curve
through memory and shadow
rhythms stumble and stop,
come again, the night air a willing audience.

men huddle near a long, brass bar rail,
shoes gleaming, lips smiling, eyes lit
as women, young and old, stroll pass them
on their way to the powder room

las mujeres motion a dream of sand and waves
a Cuba that only the restaurant owner
and his waiters may have truly seen, heard.

late winter, rains slicking the streets of lower Manhattan,
Son Cubano's portals reveal a theater of nostalgia
the scent of Havana scripts so well.

And we play along
mouths flavored with rum, lime, sugar, our tongues playing
the *kisses stolen game* as the song phrases
a fierce sadness promised
in the wake of lust's mercurial ascent
We flee these orchestrated memories

our hands in each others, our mouths hungry for each other.

Our song is bluer, harsher, North American
the rhythms African, yes, as dearly measured in drama and depth.

Our exile is internal. There is little longing
for the good old days when Havana was a mean place
for dark people, but a real fascination
for these songs and their makers.

Your arms cascade a trumpet solo, the piano's
harmonics thrill my back.
My lips are waiting for yours.

This is our *bolero*
accidental
lovemaking   Friday night   New York City
Everybody's exotic.

Everybody's from the South.

L'affaire est finie

Oh how *faux* proverbial
when one door opens
another almost always stays shut
                    (you)

PUMP

Somewhere, the devil rallies we shefolk fast before sunrise
and the knives that set quiet in their berths suavely
rise to find chests and stomachs of husbands, lovers.

Raymond Chandler slouches his favorite hat smiling.
He knows a woman's heart, how weather met the rise and fall
of that pump that slurred her vision and ate away at girlish dreams.

Heat and ice. The price of stockings. What turns when the leaves die.
Crying and drinking and walking the side streets of exalted cities.
Moon howling is never enough.

Half moon over Harlem, half my heart healing
other half pumping   last grasp of anger
a politician's handshake.

Thus, the new century finds bar chatter foolish and men on cell phones
making the next date, daring to start anew what has been done
and done to death. Sweet talk storm wisdom flung on the floor

like expensive lingerie.

Trabajan la sal y el azucar/ Construyendo una torre blanca?

—Pablo Neruda

Do salt and sugar work to build a white tower?
No, they do not speak to each other.

Salt and pepper are masons
building
the perfect blank
a beautiful stark

White on white walls thick—whole cities surrounded with
lustrous black roadways—jeweled paths daunt

It is curiosity Senor Neruda that forms the white foundations
that rise platform after platform floor by floor into air—

Tower as look out.
What is seen—the enemy approaching? Or

Lot's wife dissolving—myth and punishment
elevator and aperture—the eye apparent.

But where are their tools?   put aside for dazzle

2.

Sugar tastes like sex, surprise
Salt and pepper become sun and water or lobby and floor.

Oh these white towers spiced with story, precarious
platform after platform, floor by floor falling into ruin, reverie—
blanco, *negro*, mustard, sienna, and beryl.

Spirit

wind rise, wind fall
trouble find you
trouble leave you
trouble return

love too
inside you
then gone
love returns

spectre
haint
ghost in house
loved one lost

to gun
to knife
to poison
to strife

body gone

troubled or calm
spirit remains
velvet on skin
voluptuous hurricane

THREE

I don't want his things to see me.

—FANNY HOWE, GONE

WHAT I HAVE NOT DONE FOR LOVE

I have not torn my hair in a public place
Or worn a dress the size of a dime

Once I spoke in a French accent, but it sounded
Lithuanian

I have not denounced my family
or let the back of my hand slap a cousin's cheek

I have not found the perfect strand of pearls
Or made a gift of sudden beauty
I have yet to consult
the Fortune Telling Chicken
in Chinatown

I admit a fondness Jack Daniels and Cosmopolitans
And the ease with which *Arkansas* wrecks my
my quick New York speech

On nights when stars brightly pattern the Brooklyn sky
I search for your hand and find a drift of wind.

LETTER TO ALICE

I'm up in Squaw Valley—yes the name is utterly inappropriate
in these late twentieth century days, but hey, history
isn't pretty especially place names.

Monument Valley has no monuments.
The Eiffel Tower or *Tour Eiffel* just stands there
Squat on the ground, then rises grid and girders.

The difference between New York and Paris are landmarks.
A tower for tourists. A bridge connecting boroughs.
You can walk on both, but where does that tower take you?

But back to you. Your poetry is now in the hands of critics
far flung. Like starlings they peck at loaves of text
forgive the metaphor

I know you must find this thrilling or pitiful depending on
the tenor of gray that manifests itself as Parisian sky
Light gray—mist, darker gray—rain, rain, rain.

Thinking about the Myth of Alice Notley
Everyone want just that touch of your Irish wit, if indeed,
and your whiplash phrasing, like Ornette Coleman off the stars.

I was like thinking of you riding the Second Avenue bus
Schlepping kids clothes, groceries, slips of paper with this fragment
or that dream, a poet's eye on the world, floating by—

the office building where Planned Parenthood used to be,
the bland, yet ugly, modernist Episcopal Church,
the dull gray high rises, a Synagogue, seemingly empty

the skinny boys carrying guitars weary from drink and doubt.
But this is my Second Avenue. Circadian, humbler, noisy
And full of mysteries unraveling. Yours is different.

Your Second Avenue is more home, no mystery, just the late
Supper needed fixing or another poet in town to entertain
between mothering and marriage and raving metaphors to be tamed.

My Second Avenue is for checking in and checking out
Away from the wrench of too many other hungry babypoets
angling for the teacher's glimpse, the mentor's tease.

It is a Second Avenue of bland buildings and skinny boys dangling guitars
And the phrases of Frank O'Hara, something planetary and there is no
Howard Da Silva look alike on my bus. Just the usual mutterers and weary

Ones ready for television and a really good soak.
When next we meet, it will be good to gossip. Forget our woes.
Fog softens contours. Sun bursts clarify grids and girders.
Tower and Bridge.

Give my regards to *Tour Eiffel*. It's twin, the Brooklyn Bridge, makes memory
easier to hear. Those footfalls across the East River walking away from Manhattan
across Brooklyn, the Atlantic, on to the tenth arrondissement. A café, some wine,
and your laughter.

Note to Maureen 4/25/99

Polar bear
Poet
ink and thin paper
envelop flap, adhere

Oh note, go forth into the four elements
                                no mention of hate
                                nor the millennium
                                or a line of credit that can never be repaid

any letter reads nicely
friend to friend

pity sing the old woman crooned
in that O'Connor story
just before the bad guy blew her away

grateful for fact of my own address.
I'll mail a letter any day

FAILED GHAZAL

My Brooklyn living room smells like roses and ginger—summer gardens and
    Chinese takeout
1975 San Francisco's Chinatown ginger cookies thin and spicy my tongue
    snapped sweat

That taste. I searched New York's Mott and Mulberry streets in vain for the
    same sweet heat.
Nostalgia and fear catches my throat. November.
Two hundred broken and drowned bodies in the Atlantic Ocean,

Arkansas heroine, Daisy L. Bates gone finally, one tiny paragraph in *People*
    Magazine
and so too, my good friend Peter Dee. Suddenly

I can see the morning glories encircling the window of his apartment in the
    West 80's.
Framing a room where a man a bed a typewriter performed a constant,
    caffeinated dance.

He sculpted poems and plays where his characters, many of them children
took chances large and small to find ways to be tender, loving, despite
    abandonment, despair, the world, the world, the world.

Singing voice on answering machine, demanding notes to come for tea,
    and at Christmas
those loud and splashy decorations in an apartment shoebox size, but what a
    big, big shoe.

Sam Cooke is singing *Lil Red Rooster* and the organ sways an ocean of
   comment
I can hear Peter say something smart or foolish and play again his heart's
   own way.

Child like was he alive in the moment prepared to grow within the spirit
that gives breath its business and blood its dance

And we are drinking margaritas—his really big and mine girl size, just right.
   We are
celebrating successes small, private, hard won. I want to cry. Having once
   seen his skinny legs in hospital.

Naked. I had never seen him naked and there he was sick in hospital.
And everyone on the ward loved him. His anecdotes, his silly jokes echoed
   across the big Veteran's Administration ward

down the hall, into the nurses lounge. His smile would not go away.
He knew that whatever happened, he was alive in each moment, and that

the people he loved would be okay. We will find our paths to mercy,
to those morning glories—semaphores of grace.

Notes for the Poem, "Beloved of God"/
A Memory of David Earl Jackson

At David Jackson's birthday party, the d j played funk songs and early disco,
as we stylish and sweating swayed our hips and shrieked the end of winter air.

Crossing the half century—who is still here and who has gone—drugs,
AIDS, congenital heart failure, cancer, gunshot wounds

Wine dropped on the floor in remembrance.
As we stepped towards the uncertain future of gracefully aging
or going out raging like rivers in Canada.

Amadou Diallo will never have to worry about gray hair
or creaky knees, his children's tantrums or the daily rituals of
teeth cleaning or praises to Allah.

His is a life forever fixed by 19 bullets bursting toxins
and shutting forever down his heart, his lungs, his spleen, his brain.

Eyes shut, limbs limp, lying in his essence flowing out
towards the lit stage set that has become the vestibule of his last home in

America. Where every other Black man seems to be a suspect
as he walks wearily from subway stop to home front at least in New York City.

I now know why I have always respected aging Black men.
To have defied the bullets ever ready to find their targets,
these are men of immeasurable *luck*. The sixty-something gentleman
on the 4 train, Friday morning, his voice still Georgia rich, schooling

a younger Black man. His voice rising in anger even as his suit and
suave chapeau bespeaks a man of some power—lawyer, business executive.
"They don't want you to live." And everyone knows who "they" are in his lexicon.

Here we are at the start of a new century, in the Year of the Dragon,
and we look back to a tangled history of blood desires and blood letting
or denial and lies. The violent consequences of white supremacy—four young men
raised in fear and marked by badge and gun with the chance to

lose sight of mission and common sense in the shadows of a doorway
where every boogeyman story crystallizes in the body, mind and heart of a
young African man doing nothing in particular.

They have an acquittal that is not worth the paper it's written on
and the loyalty of their brothers in arms. But who cares. They murdered.
They know it. And, so do we. What are we are to make of it?

How are we to school ourselves? Fight the power. Carry wallets.
March, riot, boycott, scream?

We live. We do not become so foolish that we think we cannot change the world.
We remain as open to new ideas and as defiant of old expectations as that aging man,
still angry and still working to make a difference that I heard on the No. 4.

Savoring the beauty of noise, gossip, anxiety and joy,
We pour libations and we remember who has been sacrificed and why.
We celebrate a half century of moving on *terra ferma*,
dancing away from the bullets.

Beloved of God

Dixie cups and bullet marks—a man's body gone to the morgue,
tiny bombs exploding limbs, organs. Bullet marks and Dixie cups.
A winter scene suddenly hot with summertime choler.
A young man's gone to Paradise.

His body is bomb site.
His assassins out of breath, out of control, out of depth.
What was there, what scent? One night
one light going out, one noise that did not sound right.

41 bullets across the plane of his body. 41 bullets scattered dust and the smell
of snow.

Alive, thinking about what—the rent,
a party, the pretty girls that did or did not smile his way.

Then the fusillade.
Amadou, Amadeus, Beloved of God. Gone to Africa, back to glory.

The fusillade. Beloved of God. Young men, young women shout your name.
Justice plucks off her dirty blindfold, joins the hue and cry.

Beloved of God. Prince of the city. Scion of Africa.
Sweet face. Hardworking. Laughing. Friendly. Biding his time.

Dixie cups cloak the breathe of damage, the depth of duty
four white men walking away. Alive. Bullets spent

What rent their good sense from finger on the trigger?
The easy gift of gun and badge?

Light bulb shatters. Someone falls as if shot. Another shoots
and this young man whispers I am free here. I am free here.

His mother will bring her sweet voice, her steely spine and her beautiful angry eyes
to bear on the city he had grown to call home. Beloved of God. Bombed body.

His father will shelter his final journey back to Africa in a shroud of pride and rage.
Beloved of God.
Gone to glory. Gone to Paradise.

Away from this most predictable of American stories—.
41 times across the hardscrabble of a Bronx street, bullets patter

like marbles, four killers walk away, tears in their eyes, perhaps.
Justice, re-knots her dirty blindfold across dull eyes,
giving them room to breathe—
A Black man dead,
Four white men walking home
again.

FEVER, BONES, BREATHE

In her hospice bed
flushed pink with fever and struggle
Ann became
a newborn bird

her skin feathered
sweat (soft)
bones thinning
(calcium disappearing)

how hard her lungs and mouth
worked (open)

 dragging air

in memory of Ann Beckerman

Valentine's Day, 2001

oddly enough
she'd finished eating the wildebeest—it took all night

former lovers cursed her shoes
all other dreams

came true
Fire and spit, roasting the beast
heat, not enough

white hairy belly subway morning
every body hot

Chinese government fakes the immolation of martyrs
Fulan Gong members hand out fliers

wind harsh, snow not much
hairy belly subway morning, he's addicted to display

her mouth is wet with half cooked beast
her mouth is wet with hair
her mouth is licking white hairy belly subway morning

Air is snow.
Free Tibet banners slung along Second Avenue
Fulan Gong members hand out fliers.

She dreams a feast and then the flat bellied man appears
subway morning her bloody mouth, the wildebeest.

Fire and spit

Who is free?
She?
Plump red valentines dangle Grand Central.
Huge bouquets in big metal buckets stand ready for plucking.

Mouths bloody. Hot meat. Hairy belly. White
subway morning. Work.

Morning ride. Grand Central orifices enclose and release
woman satisfied. Fulan Gong hands out fliers.

Chinese government fakes martyrs' deaths.
Fire in the valentine
plump red restless.

Bloody mouth. Air is ice. Street is ice.
Radiant curbside, the beast growls.

TRACE

voice activated
who might I hear?

virtual man
dreamed lover
or dream boat
tipped over

drowned man
gasping

tape re-winding

FOUR

As a child I believed pain was erasable.

—Peter Covino
Cut Off the Ears of Winter

Pain is the body's grinding.

—Fanny Howe, Gone

THREE GEMS

Amethyst for encouragement
Debbie's kind, tired voice on telephone
early morning, keeping me alive
thankful, am I

the Japanese beetles are passionately swarming
a mating dance in Virginia grasses. They bounce against our skin, glinting.
Bergamot, lavender, summer hay perfume my nighttime walk

There is mercy. It comes when needed like a red moonrise.

Obsidian for power
She said you said you were in control of your life.
Oh really, when did I say that

Well you speak with such confidence, she said. I laugh. It seems
as if I have the power to control my sliver of the great cosmic order.
Well, no. But, what little power have I, is hard won and precious. Black.

Carnelian for security
There has not been one moment in my life that was not compromised.
Lack of money or love or grander dreams, perhaps, strange luck. And now
as my body radically changes, I am anchored by strong spirit. What's up
with the sun?

And when did I turn my cheeks toward heat?

HOW HE KNOWS ME

How he knows me
comforts me

It's that we were lovers once thing
It's that we may be lovers again thing

Or simply we love

How he knows me
panics me

Stops me from trusting my own story

How she risked much
Lost a little
Got some things
back

Where I watch my tongue
is how I hear new birds

They are louder
their music stubborn

like believing in the end of things
When we are breathing.

Charming Gentleman/fever broken

He has a plan for handling volatile emotional gear.
He shares it with like-minded fellows in bars and Starbucks.
Between the whiskeys or the lattes, they nod in agreement
and plot their own version of events

Sparks fly from his shoes
Dew drops off his brow

He's trouble because he's so easy to please
or teas, my sometimes sweet man
Oh, but he's someone else's good time man.

Human stories have shapes that are hard to damage.
Triangles may be divine or soap opera,
Defined by bodies and timing.

It's not all tears and stupidity
If it was only these, there'd be no poetry

And yet, as the pear trees lining Sterling Place shiver
his musk rises from out of a fever and there's no stopping
the memory of an amazing fuck.

It's all good. For the moment (s). All good. Until a phone call
or an encounter in the wrong place. Discretion and dignity
and good home training come to play. There will be no hussy business here:
only a smart movement of La Regina, honorable in her own way.

Business is business and love can be an asset or a deficit.
It depends on smile, guile, the pluck of a woman
who plans for her future without ALL THIS DRAMA.

She's got game. She's got her heart. She's standing at the bar
beautiful, serene.

Gift in hand and ready to say,
Farewell, been good to let you go.

Aubade

Your right hand is infant like—balled fist
holding heart's sound

Last night's drink stole your tongue's usual ease
And yet you brought a storm moving faster, harder
inside me, and yes again, my heart was taken.

I watch you wake and move away
not even tears this time.

A Mocking Bird makes his presence known
across Brooklyn's backyards

Your hands open and stroke my torso
Your mouth found mine at midnight

Now your mouth is dry from all that tasting, all that wine.
This morning both our faces rough from poor sleeping.
This is the slow unraveling, the backslide we knew could happen.

Your face has quieted, the boy more present than the man,
and my heartache diminishes, more woman than the girl.
Fooling around in the dark, ours is a music of mutual solos.

By dawn's light we begin again to practice wisdom.
My neighbor's radio screams bad news.

You leave.
I go to work.

Blue Saturday

1.
This is that cold spring we did not desire.
This is that cold spring of leaves a green too delicate to describe.
This is that cold spring that will summer heat welcome

Where's my Valium,
my Percodan
my Opium
My lover's mouth and who is he kissing?

2.
He's in Seattle, San Francisco, Milwaukee, Syracuse,
He's far from the blues
In Kalamazoo ordering room service contemplating his next move
In Chicago dodging the moon, the stars keeping his eyes on the road
He's on video, radio, in the air
He's in my hair.

3.
See how swimmers return to the same lane
Winners in the water, but on land
Awkward, uncouth.

A woman's deep voice roils chlorinated water—that's what loss
can do—turn soprano into baritone; brown eyes to blue

A country tune circa 1972—is this me?

4.

The actress is blonde and skinny and actually sweet
Waiting her turn in the bathroom line, we talk
Chekhov, the Wooster Group and pray there's toilet paper
How passion divides is central to the plot, any plot
worth its time in our hands—read, seen, sung.

Swung from laughter to tears, in art, is not so easy to do.
All that sentiment, those tears, clever quips to disguise
this ordinary sadness. Lorenz Hart I thank you.

With thanks to Maria Bello—the actress

Riffing off Billie Holiday—
Saturday, the Clouds are dark again

It's that "I know what I am talking about and damn it
I wish I could change it, but I can't" understanding of the world.

Why is the world comprehensible?

What say you young woman singer, waiting for those dollars to turn into purses,
 jewels, gowns, shoes and fur? What say you young woman singer,
staunching vomit that rises from a stomach full of bad liquor and dead animals?
What say you in tune with the times, Honey?

These times deserve love ballads that swing with rhythms
learned on the playground or better yet in the womb.

Why we here? What we do? Who gives a good God _____.

And this is just a preamble.

You live long enough to see some things work and others fall to the floor,
shatter, and then you clean up the mess.
That's what adults do, clean up the mess. If they are good adults,
they clean up the mess. And go on.

But what if you're a bad adult? Or not an adult at all?
What if you're a voice and you want to get high?
And you don't give a good _____

about it? What if you're a legend, an icon?

What if you throw off a vivid perfume and clamor for the dancer's silver
shoes? Who are you when you're not so spicy?
Who are you when you sit in the big white tub purging perfume?
Who are you when you shake away the blues?   Last of the

bright lights? Are you still a bright light?
Those pearly rings, that diamond casket.

The air is full of words and you didn't write them.
The air is full of dust. Your body shedding.

You want to be a snake, beautiful, cool,
capable of natural resurrection.

No Christ in sight. No heaven to speak of.
But, no hell.

BLUE SKIES
(THE MOVIE, 2 SONGS AND THE REAL THING)

Bing Crosby did a great job in one of those thankless roles from the late 40s
When way past his prime, he played swain to an ingénue, blonde, wholesome,
easily forgotten, but the song's minor key sweetness lingers

The painted backdrops made his slightly balding seducer that much more surreal
It would have been better if he were a Lothario. Someone petty, vain and generously
bitter from past affairs done in. Done for. Or possibly he would have welcomed

this wild music coming off my CD player, Tori Amos singing/yelping
blue skies like some crazed doll whose voice box is stuck
Blue skies   blue skies   blue skies

And here am I, wide blue skies so near, clouds seem touchable.
And where are you? In my waking mind, in my real need for deep sleep.

Losing you has left me stranded, strained. Bing's handsome voice rolls
Berlin's melody along a trail of need that popular music somehow meets
so easily, like the perfect fit of English velvet gloves.

Selective memory loss comes with advanced dreaming.
I must give the potion for forgetfulness time to work. Blue skies, blue skies,
blue skies help me dream a new memory.

A LOST KEY

The 11th Street wall of St. Vincent's Hospital is covered in *Have you seen?*
Photoshop portraits and bios carefully typed or scrawled quickly
Have you seen?
Notations from the living, the loving, the despairing
Have you seen?

The Book of the Dead is wide open:
"loves music, loves fashion, loves sports—hockey, tennis, the Knicks!
loves to help others, loves his (her) job,
loves me, loves me, loved me"

Roses candles heartfelt messages

All across downtown Manhattan modest memorials bloom
In front of churches, fire houses, at Grand Central, police stations, on fences
—the *Misericordia* of modern life—how different from the harsh calculus
    of private hatred
and military precision made manifest on a September day of startling beauty

Skyline reshaped, lives lost in seconds.
In

seconds.

Left behind are stacks of books, bracelets, coffee cups, socks,
shoes dusted white—ghost commerce.
And this token of what may have been a comfortable life.
                                        dropped in haste, tossed
                            into ashy air?

THE DEVIL'S PAINTBRUSH / ILE DE LA CITE

If there was a way to bring the Devil's Paintbrush to the *Ile de la Cite*,
amazement would follow.

Wildflower is a word not usually heard on either side of the *Seine*.
What flourished on the Paris plain has long been cultivated, shifted

by commerce, tradition, the Empire's Saturnine greed. But the same sun that
warms
this North American valley where the Devil's Paintbrush flourishes with the
oxeye daisy,
clover, chicory and the invading loosestrife, hovers near the *Ile de la Cite's*
lavish chronicle.

We stand in a world where God's gifts, although terrible, are human refined:
the *Galarie des Chimieres*, the rose windows radiant, the iron gateways to and from

the Lord's Big House. Nuns in gray and white habits, skinny boys on motorcycles,
and uniformed African school children fan away from the stony growl of the great

masons quarried creatures. These gargoyles have survived six centuries of
political calamity, befoulment by fire and air, even respectful juvenile imagery
of Disney cartoons.

How would this Cathedral welcome an imagined offering: bright orange petals—
open, effervescent, summer's enticement.

MY ANGEL #1

My angel refuses to be like the others
He removed his wings and is not on television

He's a "he" which I find ironic
But then, to be spiritual in an age of religious
fundamentalism is to be ironical

My angel leaves spider webs undisturbed.
He traces tears and claims salt from the sweat of pyramid builders
He has a droll sense of humor—he's my angel.

I often think that if he were human, I'd marry him.
But his immortality keeps us apart. It's such an old story.

As for now, I am grateful for his ability
to capture curses before they make their way
towards my soul.

MY ANGEL #2

Sings with me in the shower. Our duets are pretty crazy.
I still sing alto, but I want to sing soprano. I want to carry melody

My angel laughs at my desire and allows me the occasional
Cracked note.

My angel walks with me in the Brooklyn Botanic Gardens.
He is fond of the blue bell's scent and shares my love of bamboo's
suavity. We listen to the stone coyotes that guard the Inari Shrine.
My angel is respectful of angels of all faiths.

When the first daffodils opened in March 1993, my angel let me walk
the four blocks from my apartment to Daffodil Hill, welcoming me back
to wholeness. All that yellow and the cool Spring air.

Bold or bossy or quietly shining, my angel wears his welcome.
Humming, you need protection. You need righteous air.

After Nina Zivancevic

Second Night, New Home—12/05

Was it midnight
Or earlier, the day not done

How the soft voice of a friend in need
Danger
Love
It is late and the world is exhausted.

Notice: no dream here.
Real Life is minute by minute
Task by task
Kiss by kiss
Or the flashing neon William Hopper painting world post-structuralists flee
Those simulacra

are much easier to tease the footnotes out of.
OH PLEASE OH PLEASE OH PLEASE

Follow colors from one room to the other, thankful.
There is no water, no wind, no criminal ready to flood, flag or flay me.

Just a midnight call, a mistake, misdeed
a missed opportunity to connect past promises
to future pleasures or is it the other way around?

I am exhausted.
Eyes puff up
Lord is sung in a million tongues

I pray. Allow me a fearless darkness.

ERA VERDAD AQUEL AROMA/
DE LA DONCELLA SORPRENDIDA

—PABLO NERUDA

Was it true (real) that scent of the surprised maiden?
Who would know, but her lover, his tongue exploring
those generous lips between her legs

Suddenly knowledgeable of her treasure and loss
breath rises and falls growing stronger to stay
her Venus ascends and his scent grows
a forest of toadstools, brambles, roots digging
eating the rot and riot of forest floor.

How genial they are—sex and sympathy,
Simpatico, a word, you knew too well, Maestro
Your tongue at play with many a maiden,
surprising many a matron.

How nature surprises each of us
Peach taste
Fish flapping
Hurricane reshaping North Carolina's Outer Banks

Moss, flowers, ferns erupt those walks across Isla Negra
Voicing a verdant earth encircled by desire

Sought
Found
Lost

and found again.

CHRISTMAS SEASON, 2004

As a walking flood—seventy percent water—ready to spill blood
at the corner, in a kitchen, another image on the flat screen TV

As a walking flood, dry land matters.
As a walking flood, summits attract.

Hill tops, tree tops, the roofs of houses:
slanted, sodden, flat enough for helicopters.

What we cling to when our bodies encounter heavier water,
damaged wind, the sparkle of bombs' tracings

on streets as far or near
as the names given

By whom
when earth shifts and time speeds up.

We slosh and sway in streets with names given
To meet our need for comfort
Wine, food, lovers' kisses

Wet things
Slippery
Soft

Then harsh enough
To flash our names away

CODA

Last day of Passover, April 2006

It is one of those soft days, girls are snapping gum
And flinging their scent-
Boys look their way defiant interested and if you see them at a certain angle
  terrified.

Oh New York City, eternal dramas of teenagers in love lust mad
Money in this whirl

And their Mamas and Papis tired. Long days at the MTA the office the factory
That will close sometime next year globalization builds up one set of poor people
Tears down another.

And why am I listening to Milton Nascimento unfolding a silk curtain
of sounds Brazil, the late 1970s the world dreams a freedom
for Africans in the New World,
north and south and Milton is one
to sing those dreams to me. Oh Saxophone. Oh Trumpets.
Oh rhythms Southern African Indian the New World honored.
Oh first kisses and last goodbyes.

I pray for friends in grief their Mamas and Papis sick and dying.
I pray for my own heart stunned too often by love's promise, then
Left to heal somehow.
I pray for you now gone, more than a year.
Many days and nights long ago, we parted
Our New Orleans washed away

Washed away.

Someone some where burn some sage for me
Drums liberate senses remember
Remember

Spring is the season that demands an abandonment of innocence;
Demands we tease out sadness from our petty hormonal clowning

Demand we walk among the ghosts our hopes
Calling fierce names, soft names, loved names, lost names

In language as liquid as Portuguese or as supple as English.

In memory of Ahmos Zu-Bolton

"What the First Cities Are All About." The Metropolitan Museum of Art in New York City hosted Art of the First Cities: The Third Millennium B.C. from the Mediterranean to the Indus in 2003, the year America invaded Iraq. The napkin reference is to "Poem #12" in The *Poems of Catullus* translated by Charles Martin.

"Son Cubano" is a musical motif in Latin Music and the name of a Cuban restaurant in the Meat-packing District of Manhattan on W. 14th Street

Poems whose titles are from *Preguntas* by Pablo Neruda were collected in *repuestas!*, a chapbook. *Repuesta* is the Spanish word for answer.

"Letter to Alice" is dedicated to Alice Notley and "Note to Maureen" is dedicated to Maureen Owen.

"Failed Ghazal" is an elegy for Peter Dee, the Boston-raised, New York based Irish American playwright who wrote "Voices From The High School" and "Amber Patches." He died in October, 1999.

NOTES FOR THE POEM, "BELOVED OF GOD"/A MEMORY OF DAVID EARL JACKSON. Originally from Chattanooga, Tennessee, Jackson was an African American poet, writer, cultural and political activist. He died in August 2001.

"Beloved of God "is dedicated to Amadou Diallo, an African immigrant gunned down by policemen in February, 1999. He was 23 years old.

"Riffing off Billie Holiday—Saturday, the Clouds are dark again" was written a week before the re-election of George W. Bush in 2006.

"Blue Saturday" Lorenz Hart was the lyricist half of Rodgers (Richard) and Hart. Together they created popular Broadway shows during the 1920's; 30s and early 40s including *Babes in Arms* and *Pal Joey.* Hart died in 1943. .

"Second Night-12/05" was written after moving to Bedford Stuyvesant after living for 14 years on Sterling Place in Prospect Heights, Brooklyn

"Last day of Passover, April 2006" The Milton Nascimento album is *Encontros E Despididas (Encounters and Farewell).* An earlier poem Encounter and Farewell about Ahmos Zu-Bolton is in *The Weather That Kills.*